The Yearling

Marjorie Kinnan Rawlings

D1614297

Level 3

Retold by Coleen Degnan-Veness

Series Editors: Andy Hopkins and Jocelyn Potter

Pearson Education Limited
Edinburgh Gate, Harlow,
Essex CM20 2JE, England
and Associated Companies throughout the world.

Pack ISBN: 978-1-4058-5217-3
Book ISBN: 978-1-4058-5077-3
CD-ROM ISBN: 978-1-4058-5078-0

First published in the USA 1938
First published by Penguin Books 2001
This edition published 2007

3 5 7 9 10 8 6 4

Original copyright © Marjorie Kinnan Rawlings 1938
Text copyright © Penguin Books Ltd 2001
This edition copyright © Pearson Education Ltd 2007
Illustrations by Joisé María Rueda

Set in 11/13pt A. Garamond
Printed in China
SWTC/03

Produced for the Publishers by AC Estudio Editorial S.L.

*All rights reserved; no part of this publication may be reproduced, stored in a retrieval system,
or transmitted in any form or by any means, electronic, mechanical, photocopying,
recording or otherwise, without the prior written permission of the Publishers.*

Published by Pearson Education Ltd in association with Penguin Books Ltd,
both companies being subsidiaries of Pearson Plc

Acknowledgements
We are grateful to the following for permission to reproduce photographs:
The Kobal Collection: Page 74 © Anne-Marie Weber / CORBIS; page 75 (tr) (20th Century Fox /
Paramount), (m) (Universal), (l) (20th Century Fox)
Picture research by Karen Jones
Every effort has been made to trace the copyright holders and we apologise in advance for any
unintentional omissions. We would be pleased to insert the appropriate
acknowledgement in any subsequent edition of this publication.

For a complete list of the titles available in the Penguin Active Reading series please write to your local
Pearson Longman office or to: Penguin Readers Marketing Department, Pearson Education,
Edinburgh Gate, Harlow, Essex CM20 2JE, England.

Contents

1.1 What's the book about?

1 Look at the picture on page 43 and talk about it. What can you guess about the boy, his home, and his feelings for the fawn?

2 Put these animals in the correct group.

bear

horse

cow

hog

dog

rattlesnake

deer

a They work on the farm where the boy lives. ....dog,..

b Their meat or milk is food for the boy and his family.

....

c They are very dangerous. ....

1.2 What happens first?

Look at the pictures on pages 1–11. What do you think? Circle the correct words.

1 The story happens in the 1890s / 1990s.

2 It starts in winter / spring.

3 The boy, Jody, lives on a farm in Alaska / Florida.

4 He lives with his mother and father / brothers and sisters.

5 He goes out to look for a bear / deer.

CHAPTER 1

Jody's First Water Wheel

"He should run! He should build water wheels!
One day, he'll stop being a boy."

There was a thin, straight line of blue smoke coming from the little house in the woods. As the smoke reached the blue April sky, Jody watched it change from blue to gray. His mother was hanging up the pots after the noon dinner. He was thinking, "She'll wash the floor after she sweeps it. So, she won't miss me if I go down by the river."

Jody looked across the field of **corn**, put down his **hoe** and started walking. It was spring and the corn could wait another day. He jumped over the **fence**. Old Julia, his father's dog, was with his father in Grahamsville. But Rip and Perk saw him and ran after him. Their tails **wag**ged happily when they saw him. But Jody sent them back to the yard.

Jody thought, "Those two dogs are good for nothing except **hunt**ing deer. They like me only when they're hungry. Old Julia's a good dog, but she's **Pa**'s dog.

corn /kɔrn/ (n) long, yellow vegetables that come from a tall plant
hoe /hoʊ/ (n/v) a long tool for taking unwanted plants from the ground
fence /fens/ (n) something of wood or metal that is put around an area of land
wag /wæg/ (v) to shake from side to side
hunt /hʌnt/ (v/n) to follow animals, usually because you want to kill them
Pa /pɑ/ (n) an old word for *father*

deer

buck

doe

fawn

bear

squirrel

cow

calf

hogs

fox

rabbit

rattlesnake

raccoon

I want one that's mine. I want one that'll kiss me with his little pink tongue." But, Jody thought sadly, "**Ma** hates pets. To her, they're just more mouths to feed."

The road dropped below him twenty feet—down to a little stream. This was a secret, lovely place. The stream joined Lake George—a part of the St. John's River. This great river went north and into the ocean. Jody felt excited, looking at the beginning of the ocean. He liked to think, "Only me and the wild animals come to this place."

He took out his knife and cut some long, thin sticks from a tree. He wanted to make a water wheel. Grandma Hutto's son Oliver taught him how to do it last year. "I've never made one alone," he thought. He cut small holes and pushed sticks carefully into them. It took a long time. When he finished, he put the wheel in the stream. The stream pushed it. It turned easily. "Maybe it'll never stop," he thought, as he lay down close to the water. Watching his wheel, he slowly fell asleep.

When he woke up, the sun was gone. A light rain was falling. He got up. Suddenly, he noticed the **track**s of a deer in the sand near the stream. The tracks were sharp and pointed—the tracks of a doe. They were deep in the sand, so she was large. Maybe she had a fawn inside her. He looked around for other tracks and found tracks of squirrels and raccoons.

Jody couldn't tell the time of day in the grayness. Then suddenly, the rain stopped and the sun shone again. The sky looked beautiful. Jody felt full of happiness. He was grateful to be alive. He turned and ran toward home.

They called their land Baxter's Island. It belonged to his father, Penny Baxter. Jody could hear the horse, the cow, and the dogs—they all wanted their supper. He opened the gate and ran to find his father.

Penny Baxter was standing at the woodpile. Jody saw his father's hands. They were big compared to the rest of him. Penny was picking up a pile of wood, doing Jody's work. Jody ran to him.

"I'll get it, Pa!"

"Where have you been, son? I was looking for you."

"I went down to the stream."

"It was a beautiful day for that," his father said. "When I was a boy, I liked going down to the stream, too. But your mother . . ." he said, looking at the house, ". . . your mother doesn't understand us. Women don't. She doesn't know that you weren't here. Now, go take her some wood."

Jody filled his arms with wood and hurried to the house. His mother was making supper.

Ma /mɑ, mɔ/ (n) an old word for *mother*
tracks /træks/ (n pl) signs of feet on the ground; a *track* is a path

"It smells really good, Ma. That isn't cornbread, is it?"

"Yes, it is. And it's ready, so hurry. Call your father."

Jody ran to the **barn**. His father was getting milk from Trixie, the cow.

"Must I feed old Caesar?" Jody asked.

"No, I've fed him and the dogs. Take this milk to your mother. Don't drop it like you did yesterday."

Ma Baxter sat, waiting for them. She was a large woman and her body filled one end of the table. Jody and Penny sat down.

"You hungry tonight?" she asked.

"I can eat a horse!" Jody said.

"That's what you say now. But your eyes are bigger than your stomach."

"I can eat a horse, too," said Penny. "I'm always hungry after a trip to Grahamsville!"

In winter, there was very little food on the Baxters' table. But it was spring now, and there was more food. After supper, Jody lit a **candle** so his mother could wash the dishes. He looked out the window and saw the big, round full moon.

barn /bɑːn/ (n) a large farm building where you keep, for example, animals or vegetables
candle /ˈkændl/ (n) a tall, round stick; you burn it to produce light

"Do you remember what I told you about the full moon in April?" Penny asked his son.

"No, I . . . I don't remember," Jody answered. He often forgot things.

"The bears come out of their winter beds on the full moon in April."

"And we have to catch old Slewfoot!" Jody remembered excitedly.

"He'll be fat and lazy. His meat'll be real sweet after sleeping all winter."

"When can we go, Pa?"

"When we see some signs of bear. We'll go down to the stream and look. Maybe he's gone down there for a drink."

"A great big deer was there today when I was asleep. I built a water wheel there today, Pa! It worked really well."

"So, you went down to the stream today?" Jody's mother asked.

Jody could see a little smile on her face. He ran in circles around her until he couldn't stand up.

"If you knock those plates off the table, you'll be sorry!"

Jody laughed, "Everything's going around and around."

"You're crazy!" said his mother.

It was true. Jody was crazy with thoughts of spring, and of his water wheel, the doe, his father's kindness, his mother's good food. He thought about old Slewfoot. The great black bear was probably waking up. He was probably tasting the air and smelling the moonlight right now.

Jody went to bed, but he couldn't sleep. The thoughts of this wonderful April day kept him awake. And for the rest of his life, a feeling of excitement came back to him every April when the taste of rain was on his tongue. Then a bird called across the bright night, and suddenly he was asleep.

◆

Penny Baxter lay awake next to his large, sleeping wife and he thought about his son. When Penny was a boy, he worked from morning until night. He had to carry heavy bags of corn until his little body ached. He never grew taller than a boy. Lem Forrester said to Penny one day, "You're no bigger than a penny! Little old Penny Baxter." His real name was Ezra Ezekial Baxter, but everyone called him Penny.

"Penny Baxter is either a brave man or a crazy one," people said when he took his new wife into one of the wildest parts of Florida. But for Penny Baxter,

wild animals were not as dangerous as some men. They had neighbors, the Forresters, who lived four miles away—not too close and not too far. The Forresters' sons were growing into big, strong men. They needed all the space that they could get. They were as wild as the animals around them.

Penny started thinking about the past. When they got married, he and Ory wanted a large family. Ory was a big, strong woman, but the babies were weak. Soon after they were born, they died. Finally, Jody was born when Ory was almost too old for more babies. Then, when Jody was two years old, Penny had to go to war. He took Ory and Jody to Grandma Hutto's home in Volusia. She wasn't really Jody's grandma, but they called her that. He told Ory, "I'll be back in a few months." But he didn't come back until four years later.

Jody's mother accepted her youngest child, but she wasn't close to him. All of her feelings of love were dead—like her babies. But Penny ached with the love that he felt for Jody. He wanted his son to be happy.

"If he wants to make water wheels in the stream, he'll go," thought Penny. "His mother can't stop him! He should run! He should build water wheels! One day, he'll stop being a boy."

CHAPTER 2

Old Slewfoot Wakes Up

That big bear was a personal enemy now.
Jody couldn't wait to begin the hunt.

J ody woke up and went to the kitchen. His mother was cooking breakfast and his father was outside. Suddenly, old Julia started **bark**ing excitedly. Jody hurried out the door and ran toward the noisy dog.

"Slowly, son. You won't want to see this," his father said.

Jody stopped. His father was looking down on the bloody body of Black Betsy, their best hog.

"Look carefully, son," said Penny. "Do you see what I see?"

Jody's blood jumped when he saw the tracks in the sand. They were the tracks of a very large bear. One foot had only four toes, not five.

"Old Slewfoot!"

"That's right, son," said Penny. "I'm proud that you remembered his tracks." They studied the **direction** of the tracks.

"The dogs didn't hear him, Pa," said Jody, "and I didn't either."

"That bear knew the direction of the wind. He was safe. There was no hope for poor old Betsy. Look at her, son. He killed her, but he wasn't hungry. That's why I hate bears. They kill just for sport."

"Will you take her in the barn?" Jody asked.

"The bear made a mess of the meat, but I can save some of it," Penny said sadly.

But Jody was full of excitement. That big black bear was a personal enemy now. Jody couldn't wait to begin the hunt, but he felt some fear, too.

When Ory saw Betsy, she cried, "Oh no, oh no—my best hog!"

"Old Slewfoot did it, Ma. His tracks were there."

Breakfast was on the table. They sat down, but Ma Baxter was shaking. She was too worried to eat. Jody put a great pile of food on his plate.

"We've got meat to eat for a long time now," he said.

"Meat now and none this winter," said Ma. "Betsy won't have any more baby pigs, will she?"

"I'll ask the Forresters for a hog," said Penny.

"Yes, and we'll have to be grateful to those terrible people! That bear! I'd like to pull him to little pieces!" Ma said.

bark /bɑrk/ (v) to make the short, loud sounds that a dog makes
direction /dəˈrɛkʃən, daɪ-/ (n) the way to go

"I'll tell him when I see him," Penny said calmly.

Jody started laughing.

"I'm the only serious person in this family," Ma said sadly.

◆

Ma Baxter put some food in Penny's bag while he prepared his gun. Old Julia was excited and barked happily. Penny and Jody were ready for the hunt. They walked in silence. Old Julia was sure of the way. Rip followed her and watched her. He did the same as she did. Perk, the young dog, ran here and there after rabbits. He didn't understand hunting.

Julia quickly found Slewfoot's tracks. They went this way and that way. It was difficult to walk through the **scrub**. Penny and Jody saw tracks of other animals, too.

Soon they were in the **swamp**. Penny pointed and Jody understood. Slewfoot's tracks were fresh. He wasn't far away now. Julia was ready to attack. Suddenly, she barked in that special way. It meant only one thing.

scrub /skrʌb/ (n) an area of low trees and wild plants
swamp /swɑmp, swɔmp/ (n) an area of soft, wet land

"The stream!" Penny shouted. "He's trying to get to the stream!"

The black bear ran, and the young trees in his path crashed to the ground. Penny ran as fast as he could. He lifted his gun. The dogs were on the bear, biting him. Penny couldn't shoot because the dogs were in the way. Then, suddenly the dogs moved back. The time was right to shoot. He tried, but the gun didn't work. The dogs and the bear were fighting again. Jody was frozen with fear. Then Penny shot again, but this time the gun knocked Penny to the ground. Jody ran to his father, but Penny was on his feet again.

Jody screamed, "He's killing Julia!"

Penny ran to the bear and hit him hard with the end of the gun. The bear fell. His great body went down the hill and into the deep water. Slewfoot swam madly. He reached the other side and ran.

Julia was badly hurt, so Penny carried her home.

In the night, Julia cried in her sleep. Penny got up a few times to sit with her. But in the morning, Julia was better.

2.1 Were you right?

Look back at your answers to Activity 1.2 on page iv. Then complete this information.

The Yearling
by Marjorie Kinnan Rawlings

It's the ¹ .... 1890s ....

Jody Baxter lives with his
² .... and
³ .... on a farm
in ⁴ ....

It is ⁵ .... , an
exciting time of year for Jody.

When his father leaves on a
⁶ .... hunt, Jody
goes with him.

PENGUIN ACTIVE READING
The Yearling
Marjorie Kinnan Rawlings

2.2 What more did you learn?

1 Complete the sentences with these people.

The Baxters	Jody	The Forresters	Penny	Ory	Slewfoot

a .... Jody .... really wants a pet.

b .... have only one child. Their other babies died.

c .... is happy when his son is having fun.

d .... is often worried about food.

e .... are Jody's neighbors.

f .... is a bear.

2 Does Penny kill the bear? Why (not)?

....
....
....
....

12

2.3 Language in use

Look at the sentences in the box on the right. Then make nouns from these adjectives to complete the sentences below.

> Jody felt full of **happiness**.
>
> Jody couldn't tell the time of day in the **grayness**.

kind	dark	pretty	bright	wet	sad

1 Ory's ....sadness............ about her dead babies never really left her.

2 The Baxters remembered Grandma Hutto's .... during the war, when she gave them a room in her house.

3 His eyes hurt in the .... of the afternoon sun.

4 He always enjoyed the .... of the spring flowers.

5 An animal was moving quietly in the .... of the night.

6 He could feel the .... of an animal's tongue on his hand.

2.4 What happens next?

Jody visits these people. Who do you think he *doesn't* like? Why? Make notes.

Eulalie Boyles

The Forresters

Grandma Hutto

Notes

CHAPTER 3

Business with the Forresters

Jody understood about Fodder-wing. He was born when his mother was already old. He was strange, but he was kind.

Penny said at breakfast, "We'll have more trouble if I don't get a new gun."

"How can you buy a new gun?" Ma asked.

"I didn't say 'buy' a gun," answered Penny.

He decided to visit the Forresters. He needed a new gun, and they had a lot of guns. They loved dogs, and he didn't need Perk. So, he and Jody rode on old Caesar, their only horse, through the woods.

When they arrived at the Forresters', Penny said, "Now, be nice to Fodder-wing."

"I'm always nice to him," said Jody. "He's my friend. He's my best friend, except for Oliver Hutto."

Ma Forrester greeted them. She smelled of wood smoke and pipe smoke. She and Pa Forrester had seven sons: Buck, Mill-wheel, Gabby, Pack, Arch, Lem and Fodder-wing. They were big strong men except for the youngest son. Fodder-wing hurried toward Jody. He couldn't stand up straight, and he moved like an animal with a broken foot. He lifted his walking stick and waved it. His face was one big, happy smile.

"Jody!" he shouted.

Jody understood about Fodder-wing. He was born when his mother was already old. He was strange, but he was kind. He loved animals and they loved him, too. He had rabbits, squirrels, raccoons, and a bird with a bad foot. He showed Jody his pets. Jody wanted a pet and Fodder-wing wanted to give him one. But Ma Baxter was completely different from Ma Forrester. He couldn't ask her again.

That evening, Penny got a gun and the Forresters got Perk. Everyone was happy. They invited Penny and Jody to eat with them. Jody couldn't believe his eyes. There was so much food! Penny told the men about Slewfoot, and they were as interested as dogs on a hunt.

After supper, it was time for Penny to go home. Fodder-wing wanted Jody to stay the night.

"He can stay," said Buck. "I have to go to Volusia tomorrow. I'll take him home then."

"All right," said Penny. "His Ma won't like it, but it's OK with me."

Jody followed his father to his horse. "Thanks, Pa. I haven't played for a long time. So, you've got the gun and they've got Perk. You're pretty smart, Pa. You didn't lie about Perk. He's not good on a hunt, but you tried to tell them."

"My words were true, but the meaning wasn't straight. They'll discover that Perk isn't a good hunting dog. They'll want to kill me, but maybe they'll laugh! Be good, now."

Late that night, Jody was woken by a lot of noise. Suddenly, all of the men and dogs ran into Fodder-wing's room. The men wore only their pants. Ma Forrester, holding up a candle, was in her nightdress. The dogs were running all around and barking madly. Then, they ran out of the house.

"Ma heard an animal. She can hear real well," said Fodder-wing.

"It's gone now, so let's have a drink," said Pa Forrester.

"Who can sleep now?" said Buck. "Let's have some music!"

Some of the sons played music, others sang. Jody thought, "How can Ma dislike these happy people?"

Lem said, "I need my girl here to help me sing and dance."

Jody asked, "Who's your girl, Lem?"

"Twink Weatherby," he answered.

"She's Oliver Hutto's girl, Lem," said Jody.

Lem gave Jody an angry look. "Don't ever say that again. You understand?"

CHAPTER 4

Jody Shoots his First Buck

*Jody felt sick when he saw the dead animal. "I'd like
to get our meat without killing it," he said.*

One evening, a few weeks later, Jody said, "Ma, we have plenty of milk. Can
I get a little fawn—for a pet for me? Can I?"

"Of course not. There isn't any milk at the end of the day."

"It can have *my* milk," said Jody hopefully. "I just want something—
something that's mine. I want something that wants *me*, too."

"You'll never find it," she answered impatiently. "Not from any animal and
not from any man."

Penny listened quietly from his corner.

The next morning he said, "We'll go hunt for a buck today, Jody. We'll see
some fawns. It's nice to see them in the wild. It's as nice as seeing them around
the house."

"We need more deer meat in the smoke-house," Ma said happily. Ma was
always happier when she talked about food.

They got ready, then Penny, Jody, and Julia left the house. Penny carried the
gun that he got from the Forresters. Jody carried Penny's old gun. They were
following the tracks of two bucks. After a long walk, Jody saw a doe with

its fawn. He happily watched the fawn drink its mother's milk.

They stopped for lunch, and Penny said, "The two bucks will be back this way soon if the wind doesn't change direction. You can climb up one of those tall trees and watch for them. They should get close before you shoot."

Jody sat in the tree, watching for the bucks. They came into view. He sat quietly, but nervously. When the larger buck came closer, Jody shot it. He hit it, but he didn't kill it. Then Penny shot and the buck fell down. Jody climbed down the tree and ran toward it.

"Did I hit it?" Jody asked.

"You hit him. You did a real good job. You shot a little high, but you shot him."

Jody felt sick when he saw the dead animal. "I'd like to get our meat without killing it," he said.

"Me too, but we've got to eat," said Penny. "We'll take this into Volusia. If you want, we'll give the skin to Grandma Hutto."

"She'd like that," said Jody.

"But, maybe you'd like to give it to your girlfriend," Penny joked.

"I haven't got a girlfriend—only Grandma Hutto."

"Don't you like Eulalie?"

"I hate her! If you say that again, I'll die!" said Jody.

"All right, I just wanted to be sure," Penny answered, smiling.

The sand road was long and hot, but Penny carried the dead buck easily. When they reached the St. John's River, Jody looked at the water. He thought, "It's the pathway to the world." Penny called to the man who took passengers across the river. He took them across in his boat.

Penny and Jody walked into the Volusia store. Mr. Boyles paid Penny for the deer meat. Jody looked at all of the things in the shop.

"Young man, your Pa doesn't come into Volusia very often. I'll give you anything here that costs no more than a dime," said Mr. Boyles.

"I guess that costs more than a dime," said Jody, pointing to a knife.

"Yes, it does, but it's been here a long time. You can have it."

"Thank you, sir," he said.

"He's a polite boy," Mr. Boyles said to Penny.

"He's a good boy," Penny said. "We lost so many babies. Sometimes I think that I need him too much."

Jody felt proud. Suddenly, as he looked up, he saw Eulalie Boyles. He hated her face, her hair, her teeth, her feet, and everything about her. He picked up a potato from a pile and held it tightly. She put out her tongue. Jody threw the potato. It hit her on the shoulder and she screamed.

Penny said, "Jody!"

Mr. Boyles came toward Jody with an angry face.

Penny said, "Give Mr. Boyles that knife and get out of here!"

Jody went outside into the hot sunlight. He wanted to disappear. But he wasn't sorry.

"Why did you do that?" Penny asked when he came out of the store.

"I hate her! She put out her tongue, and she's ugly."

"You can't live your life that way. You can't throw potatoes at all the ugly women that you meet."

"Don't tell Grandma Hutto, Pa," Jody said. "I'll be polite . . ."

"All right, but don't do that ever again."

Jody felt a little happier. As they reached Grandma Hutto's small white house, Jody ran down the path through the garden. He called, " Hi, Grandma!"

"Jody!" she called.

He ran into her arms and held her tight. She was happy to see Penny and Jody.

"We've brought deer meat and a deer skin for you!" said Jody.

She lifted her hands in the air. Their gifts were like gold. But, in Jody's mind, Grandma Hutto was more special than gold. All men loved her. But women usually hated her. Ma Baxter was happy to leave Grandma Hutto's house after those four years. The older woman was also happy because she and Ory Baxter were as different as night and day.

Grandma Hutto made a fine supper for Penny and Jody. She gave Jody a glass of wine. They talked until it was time for bed.

"Lem Forrester wants Twink Weatherby to be his girlfriend," Jody told Grandma.

"He'll have to fight my Oliver for her, then," said Grandma. And they all laughed.

3.1 Were you right?

Look back at Activity 2.4. Then complete these sentences.

1   Jody enjoys some music in the middle of the night with ....

2   He throws a potato at .... because he hates her.

3   .... is his favorite woman in the world.

3.2 What more did you learn?

1   **Are these sentences right (✓) or wrong (✗)? Change the sentences that are wrong. Write them below.**

    a ✓ Fodder-wing Forrester is Jody's friend.

    b ☐ Penny gets a new dog from the Forresters.

    c ☐ Lem Forrester wants the same girlfriend as Oliver Hutto.

    d ☐ Jody kills a deer.

    e ☐ Jody buys a knife at Mr Boyles's store.

    f ☐ Grandma Hutto's house is in the same town as the store.

....

....

....

....

....

2   **Who or what is described in these sentences?**

    a They were big strong men. ....

    b He was strange, but he was kind. ....

    c "He's not good on a hunt." ....

    d "It's the pathway to the world." ....

    e "He's a polite boy." ....

    f "All men loved her." ....

3.3 Language in use

Look at the sentences in the box on the right. Then complete the sentences below with these words.

> They were **as** interested **as** dogs on a hunt.
>
> She and Ory Baxter were **as** different **as** night and day.

the night sky	a bear with a hurt foot	a six-year-old at Christmas
a gun shot	the grass in springtime	one of Grandma Hutto's beds

1 Jody (excited) .....*Jody was as excited as a six-year-old at Christmas*...............

2 Ory (angry) ....

....

3 The pile of cut grass (comfortable) ....

....

4 The sound (loud) ....

....

5 The girl's hair (dark) ....

....

6 Her eyes (green) ....

....

3.4 What happens next?

Look at these pictures. What is happening in each one? What do you think? Write sentences.

1 ....

2 ....

CHAPTER 5

The Fight with the Forresters

"I can't fight the Forresters. I can't stop being friends with Fodder-wing."

Very early the next morning, the river boat woke Jody and Penny. Penny said, "The boat stopped. Somebody's coming."

Jody shouted, "It's Oliver!"

A voice outside called, "Get out of bed, you lazy land-animals!"

Grandma Hutto ran from her bedroom. Oliver lifted his mother up in the air. Penny came out and shook Oliver's hand.

"Give me those gold earrings!" said Grandma. She reached up to his ears, took them, and put them in her own ears. Oliver laughed and shook her.

"Where have you been, Oliver? What've you seen?" asked Jody.

"He wants to come in, Jody. He can't start telling stories immediately after he walks in the door," said Penny.

"That's why a sailor comes home. To see his Ma and his girlfriend—and to tell lies," laughed Oliver.

Grandma Hutto cooked a big breakfast while Oliver gave presents to everyone. There was expensive material for his Ma, **tobacco** from Turkey for Penny, and for Jody—a beautiful knife.

"Nobody's got a knife like this," said Jody, "not even the Forresters."

"That's what I thought," said Oliver. "Those black-beards can't do better than us."

Jody thought about Oliver and the Forresters. Did he have to choose between them? Without thinking, he said, "Lem Forrester says that Twink Weatherby is his girlfriend."

Oliver laughed and said, "Nobody takes my girlfriend away from me."

Jody felt better because now both Grandma Hutto and Oliver knew his secret. Then, he remembered Lem's angry face. He quickly put it out of his mind.

After breakfast, Oliver said, "I'll be back later. I've got to go and see the town."

"Are you leaving me for that little yellow-headed Twink the minute you get home?"

"Sure," said Oliver, and he touched his mother's gray hair. "Penny, you're not going home today, are you?"

---

tobacco /təˈbækoʊ/ (n) something that you smoke

"I have to. I can't leave Ory home alone for too long."

Both Jody and Grandma Hutto felt sad as they watched Oliver go. "I miss him already. He comes home and immediately goes out. It's worse than when he's away," she said.

"I hate to leave," said Penny, "but we have to go."

Jody walked along the river slowly, waiting for Penny. Suddenly, he heard Easy Ozell shouting at him, "Get your Pa, quick! Don't let Mrs. Hutto hear."

Jody ran through the garden and called his father. Penny came outside.

Easy said, "Oliver's fighting the Forresters. He hit Lem outside the store. Then, all of the Forresters jumped on him. They're killing him."

Penny ran to the store. Jody tried to follow.

"Are we fighting for Oliver, Pa?" Jody called.

"We're fighting for the man that's down. And that's Oliver."

"But, Pa, we have to be friends with the Forresters. You said that. No man can live on Baxter's Island and be enemies of the Forresters."

"I said that. But I have to stop them."

Jody thought, "It's stupid to fight because of girls. Oliver left us to see a stupid girl. This is his punishment." He thought of Fodder-wing. "I can't fight the Forresters. I can't stop being friends with Fodder-wing."

He called to his father, "I'm not going to fight for Oliver."

Penny didn't answer. The fight was in the sandy road in front of the Boyles' store. Jody saw Twink. Her face was white. Jody wanted to pull her soft yellow hair out of her head. Penny pushed through the crowd and Jody followed him.

It was true. The Forresters were killing Oliver. Lem, Mill-wheel, and Buck were on him. Jody watched. It wasn't fair—three against one. But he liked the Forresters. They sang and drank and laughed. They gave him Fodder-wing to play with. Oliver stood up and he smiled through the blood. Jody felt sick.

Jody jumped on Lem's back. Lem threw him off.

Lem shouted, "Keep out of this."

Penny called loudly, "Who's judging this fight?"

Lem said, "We're judging it."

Penny pushed in front of him.

"If it takes three men to fight one man, that one man is the better man."

Lem came toward Penny. "I don't want to kill you, Penny Baxter. But I'll knock you down if you don't get out of my way."

Penny said, "If you plan to kill Oliver, you'll shoot him like an honest man. Then you'll be murderers and die for it. But be men."

Buck looked down at the sand.

"Whose fight is it? Who has done what to who?"

Lem said, "He's come here to steal."

Twink Weatherby began to cry.

Oliver dried his face with his shirt and said, "Lem tried to steal, not me."

"So, is this the place to fight about it? Like dogs fighting in the road? You two boys can fight alone on another day."

Oliver said, "I'll fight him for what he said."

Lem said, "And I'll say it again."

They started to fight again. Penny pushed between them. Lem reached over Penny's head and hit Oliver. Soon, everyone was fighting, Penny and Jody, too. Lem pushed Jody real hard. Jody dropped into blackness.

◆

When Jody opened his eyes, he was in Grandma Hutto's house. His head ached. A sharp pain shot through his neck and shoulders. He could only turn his head part-way.

"The fight was real," he thought.

Grandma Hutto said softly, "His eyes are open."

She looked at him closely and spoke to his father. "He's strong, like you. He's all right."

Penny came to the side of the bed. He had a black eye, and his wrist was hurt. He smiled at Jody.

"We were a big help, you and me," he said.

Grandma Hutto felt carefully around Jody's neck and head. "Say something," she said. "Can you still talk?"

"Where's Oliver?" Jody asked. "Is he badly hurt?"

"He's in bed. He doesn't look so pretty now. No yellow-headed girl will look at him for some time," she said.

Grandma left the room.

Penny said, "I'm proud of you, Jody. You fought to help a friend."

Jody thought, "The Forresters are my friends, too."

Penny said, "But I guess the Forresters won't be so friendly toward us now."

Pain shot from Jody's head into his stomach. He couldn't stop being friends with Fodder-wing. Jody felt angry toward Oliver. But, it was right to help him. Too many men against one wasn't fair.

"Maybe I'll lose Fodder-wing, but I had to help Oliver." He closed his eyes. Everything was all right when he understood it.

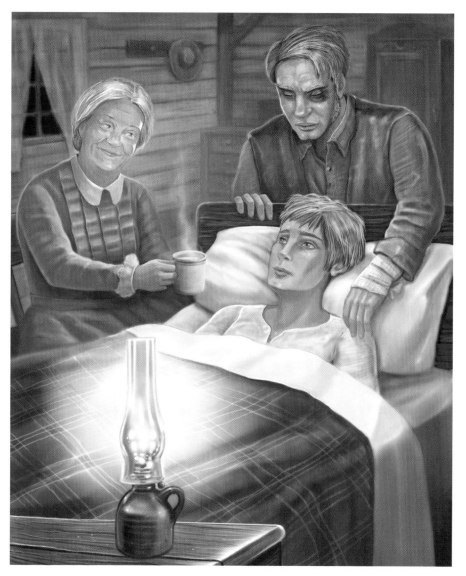

CHAPTER 6

A Rattlesnake Attack

"He bit me," he said. He looked at the two small holes in his arm.
There was a drop of blood coming out of each hole.

One day soon after the fight, the Baxters' hogs were missing. "Are you coming with me, Jody?" Penny asked his son.

Jody understood. The Forresters were angry at Penny and Jody, so they took the Baxters' hogs.

"But they'll fight us again, Pa," answered Jody. "Can't they keep the hogs?"

"Give them our meat? A black eye is better than an empty stomach."

So, Penny and Jody went to visit the Forresters. They were going through the scrub when Penny pulled a plant out of the way. Suddenly, a rattlesnake jumped out and bit him.

Penny shouted, "Get back! Hold the dogs!"

As slowly as a man in a dream, Penny stepped back. He lifted his gun to his shoulder and shot the rattlesnake. Then, he turned and looked wide-eyed at his son. He lifted his right arm and looked at it.

"He bit me," he said. His mouth was dry and moved slowly. He looked at the two small holes in his arm. There was a drop of blood coming out of each hole.

Julia made crying noises and walked away with her tail between her legs. Rip ran to the dead rattlesnake and barked loudly.

Penny started to push through the scrub. Jody ran behind him. He couldn't see where he was going. He followed the sound of his father's feet, crashing through the scrub.

Suddenly, Penny stopped. There was a doe in front of them. Penny lifted his gun and shot the doe. Jody thought, "Pa's mad to stop for deer now."

Penny ran to the dead doe and took out his knife. He didn't cut its neck, but he cut its stomach.

Jody thought, "Yes, now I know he's mad."

Penny took the doe's **liver** out of its body. He cut his own arm with his knife. Then, he put the doe's liver on the cut. In a quiet voice he said, "I can feel it." The rattlesnake's **venom** was coming out. Penny took the meat away and looked at it. It was green. He turned it and used the fresh side.

He said, "Cut a piece from the heart."

Jody jumped, took the knife and cut out a piece of heart. He gave it to Penny. Penny put it on the cut.

---

liver /ˈlɪvə/ (n) a part of your body that cleans your blood
venom /ˈvɛnəm/ (n) something from the bite or touch of an animal that can kill you

He said, "Another."

He changed the pieces of meat again and again. Then, he cut his arm again higher up where it was getting very big and very dark.

"Pa! You'll die! Does it hurt bad, Pa?"

"Like a hot knife in my shoulder."

The meat wasn't green now when he took it away. He stood up.

He said quietly, "I'm going home. Go to the Forresters. Ask them to get Doctor Wilson."

"Will they go?" Jody asked.

"We've got to try. Tell them quickly what's wrong. Maybe they won't shoot you."

Suddenly, Jody heard a noise. He saw a fawn.

"Pa! The doe's got a fawn!"

"Sorry, boy. I can't help it. Come."

Jody felt very sorry for the fawn. It walked to its mother's dead body and **bleat**ed sadly.

"Hurry!" Penny said.

Jody ran toward the Forresters'. He was afraid. "Maybe Pa'll die. Maybe the Forresters will shoot me." It was getting dark. Then he remembered Fodder-wing. "He'll help me," thought Jody.

"Fodder-wing, it's me!" shouted Jody as he ran closer to their house.

The door opened. In the light, he saw the Forrester men. They stood up, looking like great trees. Jody stopped. Lem Forrester came to the door.

"What do you want?" he asked.

"Fodder-wing . . ."

"He's sick. You can't see him."

Jody began to cry. He tried to speak. "Pa—a rattlesnake bit him."

bleat /blit/ (v) to make the weak, high sounds of a young animal, like a sheep

33

The Forresters came down the steps and stood around him. "Where is he?" they asked.

"He's walking home, but maybe he won't get there. Please get Doctor Wilson. I won't help Oliver again."

Lem Forrester laughed. "You promise?"

Mill-wheel said, "I'll get him."

"Thank you," said Jody.

"I help dogs when a rattlesnake bites them. Don't thank me."

Buck said, "I'll ride to Baxter's Island and get Penny. It's not good for him to walk."

Jody watched. Lem and Mill-wheel moved slowly. He wanted them to hurry. He felt sick with worry. He wanted to see Fodder-wing.

"Don't worry, boy," said Buck. "We'll do what we can."

Jody felt better. Maybe it was only Lem who was still an enemy. He wanted to run home, but it was four miles. So, he started walking. Soon it began to rain. The rain came down harder and harder. He couldn't run in his heavy, wet clothes. Finally, he took them off. He felt alone and afraid.

"Maybe he's dead," Jody thought. He began to cry again.

He was getting closer to Baxter's Island. When he arrived, the house was bright with light from the candles. Buck and Mill-wheel were sitting next to the fire. Jody went to the bedroom. His mother and the doctor were sitting on each side of the bed. Ma Baxter stood up and went to get a clean shirt and pants for him.

Penny's skin was dark. He was sick, but he opened his eyes. He moved his arm. It was much bigger than before.

Penny said slowly to his son, "You'll get cold."

Jody put on his clean clothes.

"That's good," said the doctor. "That's the first time that he's spoken."

It was a very long night. Everyone fell asleep except Jody. He felt alone with his father. He cried and thought, "I hate death! I don't want to be alone."

Activities 4

4.1 **Were you right?**

Look back at Activity 3.4. Then complete the sentences.

1 ..The Forresters.. fight with Oliver Hutto because Lem and Oliver like the same girl. 2 .... and 3 .... help Oliver.

_____

A 4 .... bites Penny's arm. Penny kills a
5 .... and uses the liver to take out the venom.
6 .... goes to get help from the Forresters.

4.2 **What more did you learn?**

Complete the questions and answers.

1 Why has Oliver been away from Baxter's Island .... ?
   Because he is a sailor.

2 Why .... ?
   Because it isn't a fair fight.

3 Why is Jody sad after the fight, and angry with Oliver?
   Because ....

4 Why is there a fawn alone in the woods?
   Because ....

5 Why .... ?
   Because his brothers say he's sick.

6 Why .... ?
   Because they got wet in the rain.

3.3 Language in use

Look at the sentence in the box. Then complete the sentences below, using *what*.

> "I'll fight him for **what** he said."

1 I know Lem's secret. But shall I tell anyone .....*what I know*..... ?
2 I saw the fight. I'm angry about ....
3 The illness is serious. But he doesn't say ....
4 I need some medicine. But I can't buy ....
5 He did something terrible. He'll go to prison for ....
6 They ate some food. But they didn't pay for ....

3.4 What happens next?

Choose the correct words. What do you think?

1 Penny *dies / doesn't die* from the snake bite.
2 *Jody / Buck Forrester* does the farm work that Penny can't do.
3 Jody gets a pet *fawn / dog*.
4 *Grandma Hutto / Fodder-wing* is going to give the pet a name.

CHAPTER 7

A Special Day

"Pa, I'm grown up. I don't need milk now. Can I go and find the fawn?"

Jody woke up very early. His Pa was alive, and he looked better. Jody ran to the barn and fed the animals. He got milk from Trixie. His mother poured some into a cup and took it to Penny. He was awake and smiled weakly.

"Old Death has got to wait for me," said Penny softly.

"I don't understand why you didn't die," said the doctor.

Buck and Mill-wheel came into the room and smiled.

"You aren't pretty, Penny, but you're alive," said Buck.

The doctor gave Penny the milk, and he drank it thirstily.

Penny closed his eyes and said, "I need to sleep for a week."

The doctor said, "That's what I want you to do. I can't do any more for you."

Ma Baxter said, "Who'll work the farm if he's asleep?"

Buck asked, "What work?"

"The corn needs planting."

Buck said, "I'll stay and plant the corn."

Ma Baxter looked surprised and said, "I hate to ask you."

"There aren't many of us living out here. We have to help our neighbors," said Buck.

"I'm grateful."

Then Ma Baxter went into the kitchen and made a big breakfast for the men.

"Imagine! Grateful to a Forrester!" she said to Jody.

"Buck isn't exactly a Forrester, Ma. He's a friend," said Jody.

"It seems you're right."

Jody helped his Ma with the breakfast. He talked about the doe and the fawn. During breakfast, Jody went to see his Pa.

Penny said, "I'm proud of you, son. You did what was needed."

"Pa, do you remember the doe and fawn?" Jody asked.

"I'll never forget them. The poor doe saved me."

"Pa, the fawn is out there still. It's hungry and probably really scared."

"I guess that you're right."

"Pa, I'm grown up. I don't need milk now. Can I go and find the fawn?"

"And bring it here?"

"And keep it."

Penny lay quiet, looking up.

"It won't need much. It'll soon eat plants. We took its Ma," said Jody.

38

"I'm not ungrateful. And it'll die if it doesn't get milk. My heart tells me to say yes."

"Can I ride back with Mill-wheel and find it?"

"Tell your Ma that it's OK."

Jody went to the table and said, "Ma, Pa says I can go and get the fawn."

Ma held the coffee-pot in the air. "What fawn?" she asked.

"Pa killed the doe, and it had a fawn. Pa's grateful, so he can't leave the fawn. It'll die."

Doctor Wilson said, "That's right. Nothing's free in this world. The boy's right and his Pa's right."

Mill-wheel said, "He can ride back with me. I'll help him to find it."

"If you'll give it your milk . . . We've got nothing to feed it," said Ma Baxter.

"That's what I plan to do. It won't need anything after a short time."

The doctor thanked Ma Baxter for the breakfast and left. Mill-wheel took Jody with him.

"Go north, Mill-wheel," said Jody. "Go in that direction," he said, pointing. "That's where Pa killed the doe."

"Why were you and your Pa up north?" asked Mill-wheel.

Jody thought for a minute and said, "We were looking for our hogs."

"Your hogs? Don't worry about them. They'll go home tonight, I think."

"Ma and Pa'll be happy to see them. Tell me about Fodder-wing. Is he really sick? Or didn't Lem want me to see him?"

"He's really sick. He isn't like the rest of us. He isn't like anybody."

"Can I go see him?"

"Not yet. Wait until Lem goes out one day. Then, you can see him."

"You can leave me here," Jody said. "I'll find the fawn. You can go home."

"Are you sure? There're a lot of rattlesnakes around here. Do you know the way?"

"I'll be fine. I'm very grateful. Goodbye, Mill-wheel."

Jody thought, "If it's dead, I don't want Mill-wheel to see my face."

CHAPTER 8

Jody's Fawn

It wanted to follow him. It belonged to him. It was his.
Jody felt weak with happiness.

J ody looked for the fawn. He found the body of the dead doe, but the
fawn wasn't there. There was no sound, no sign. He looked in the sand for
tracks. Under a scrub tree, he found a track and followed it.
Suddenly, something moved. The fawn lifted its head. It didn't try to get up or
run away.

Jody said softly, "It's me."

The fawn lifted its nose. Jody reached out one hand and touched the soft
neck. He felt excited and moved closer on his hands and knees. He put his arms
around its body. It didn't move. Jody stood up slowly and lifted the fawn from
the ground. It was lighter than Old Julia. Its legs were long, so Jody had to lift it
as high as possible.

When he reached the road to his home, Jody stopped. He needed a rest, so
he put the fawn down. It looked at him and bleated.

"I'll carry you again in a minute," said Jody.

Then Jody remembered his Pa's words, "A new-born animal will follow the
first person who carries it."

So, Jody started to walk away slowly. The fawn watched him. It walked a few
steps after Jody, then bleated sadly. It wanted to follow him. It belonged to him.
It was his. Jody felt weak with happiness. He wanted to play with it, run with it,
hold it. He picked it up and carried it over his two arms. He walked easily. He
was as strong as a Forrester.

Jody carried the fawn into the house, to his father's bedside.

Jody called, "Pa, look!"

Penny opened his eyes.

"It's a healthy male. I'm proud that you found him."

"Pa, he wasn't scared of me. I carried him. When I put him down, he
followed me—like a dog, Pa."

Penny looked at the fawn and said, "Little one, I'm sorry that I had to kill
your Ma."

Ma Baxter came into the room.

"Look, Ma. I found him."

"I see."

"Isn't he pretty, Ma? Look at his big eyes. Isn't he pretty?"

"He's very young. He'll need milk for a long time."

Penny said, "Ory, I've got one thing to say to you. I'm saying it now. Then, we won't talk about it again. That fawn is as welcome in this house as Jody. It's his. We'll keep him and feed him. If you get angry with Jody about this fawn, you'll have to fight with me. This is Jody's fawn, just like Julia is my dog."

Jody was surprised to hear his father speak like that to his mother.

She said, "He's young. That's all I said."

Jody made a bed for his fawn in the barn, then he went into the house.

"Fodder-wing is sick," he told his Ma.

"Is he?"

"I can't see him because Lem doesn't want me in their house. Lem is the only one who's mad at us, Ma. Mill-wheel says that I can see him. But, I have to wait until Lem goes away."

She went to the fire. As she walked past Jody, she touched his head lightly.

She said, "I feel good today, too. Your Pa's still alive."

Later, Jody took more milk to Penny. His arm was twice as big as his other arm.

"What are you going to name your fawn?" Penny asked Jody.

"I want a really special name for him."

Buck and Ma Baxter came into the room.

Penny said, "Jody needs a name for the new Baxter."

Buck said, "When you see Fodder-wing, he'll give you a name. He's good at giving names to animals. He'll choose a real pretty name."

"Go, eat your dinner, Jody," said Ma Baxter. "That fawn has taken your mind off your food."

Jody went to the kitchen. He put a pile of food on a plate and took it out to the barn. The fawn was sleepy. Jody sat with him and ate his dinner. He put his fingers in his food and held them out to the fawn. The fawn turned his head away.

"You need to learn about food. You can't drink milk all the time."

Jody finished his dinner and lay down next to his fawn. He put one arm across the fawn's neck. "I'll never be lonely again," he thought.

5.1 Were you right?

Look back at your answers to Activity 4.4. Then complete the sentences.

Penny ¹ ....doesn't die.... from the snake bite, but he has to stay in bed for a long time. While he is ill, ² .... plants the corn. Jody gets a pet ³ .... and ⁴ .... is going to give it a name.

5.2 What more did you learn?

1 Complete these sentences.

A ....Penny............ killed the fawn's mother.

B .... agrees with Penny that Jody should find the fawn.

C .... is going to bring back the Baxters' hogs.

D .... carries the fawn to Baxter's Island.

E .... is still angry with the Baxters.

2 Describe their feelings. Use some of these words.

| scared proud lonely surprised hungry grateful excited |

a Ma Baxter, when Buck offers his help on the farm ....

b Penny, about Jody's actions after the snake bit him ....

c a fawn, without a mother ....

d Jody, when he sees the fawn ....

e Jody, before he had the fawn ....

5.3 Language in use

Look at the sentences in the box. Then make similar sentences with these words, using the correct form of the verbs.

> It'll die **if** it **doesn't get** milk.
>
> Who**'ll** work the farm **if** he**'s** asleep?

1 Jody / be happy / if / he/ get / a pet

    Jody will be happy if he gets a pet

2 the Baxters / not have / enough food / if / nobody / plant / the corn

3 what / happen / to the fawn / if / we / not give / him / our milk?

4 Fodder-wing / give / your fawn / a name / if / you / ask / him

5 what / the neighbors / do / if / we / be / in trouble?

5.4 What happens next?

Jody takes his fawn to the Forresters' house. Why? What news does Buck give him when he gets there? Write your guesses.

Notes

CHAPTER 9

A Hunt with Buck

Penny shouted, "It's a bear! Get him! Get him! Quick!"
Buck ran after the bear, and Jody ran after Buck.

Jody spent a lot of time with his fawn, and his pet followed him everywhere. The days were hot and long. Penny lay in his bed, slowly getting better.

Ma Baxter couldn't believe the amount of food that Buck could eat. But, Buck was working hard and she couldn't dislike him. He was as friendly and happy as a dog.

On the eighth day, Buck said to Jody, "Look. Something has stolen some of the corn. Do you know what's done that?"

"Raccoons?" asked Jody.

"Of course not. Foxes. Foxes love corn more than I do. Two or three came last night and had a party."

"A fox party!" Jody laughed. "I'd like to see that!"

Buck didn't smile. He said, "You need to be more serious. We'll get them tonight. We'll take our guns and get them."

Jody was impatient. He couldn't wait for evening. A hunt with Buck!

That evening they heard the foxes barking. Penny gave his gun to Buck. Jody took his Pa's old gun. They walked through the cornfield. When they sawthe foxes, Jody shot one. He wanted to run and look at the fox. But Buck said, "Wait. Leave him there. Come here."

Buck gave Jody Penny's gun. "Use this to shoot the other fox."

They walked slowly, listening carefully. They saw another fox, and Jody shot it. Both foxes were dead. They carried them back to the house. But as they got closer, they heard Penny shouting.

Buck said, "Is your Ma killing your Pa?"

They ran into the yard. Penny stood in the doorway and Ma was next to him. Jody saw something. It was moving away into the dark night, and the dogs were running after it.

Penny shouted, "It's a bear! Get him! Get him! Quick!"

Buck ran after the bear, and Jody ran after Buck. At the back gate, the bear turned and Jody could see his eyes. Buck shot. The bear fell. The dogs were barking wildly. Penny came running.

Buck said proudly, "I'm a Forrester. When we hunt bears, we kill them."

"He was wild," said Penny, "because he could smell the fawn."

"Did he get the fawn, Pa? Oh, Pa, the fawn isn't hurt?"

"He never got to him. The door was closed. He came to the house, but I didn't have my gun. Ory and I couldn't do anything—just shout. But we shouted real loud and he started to run."

Jody felt weak. "My fawn's alive," he thought. He ran to the barn. The fawn was safe. Jody went back to the men and the bear. It was a two-year-old male. They took it to the back yard and took off the skin. Then, they cut it into large pieces and hung the meat in the smoke-house.

"I'll take some of the fat for my Ma," said Buck.

"Take a big piece of the liver for Fodder-wing. It'll be good for him," said Ma Baxter.

Penny said, "I'm only sad because this isn't old Slewfoot."

The excitement was good for Penny. He felt better, but soon he began to get tired again. He washed his hands, cleaned his knife, and went to bed. Buck wasn't tired. He talked to Jody, but Jody wanted to go and see his fawn. Jody closed his eyes and waited for Buck to go to sleep.

When Buck was asleep, Jody went to the barn. The fawn was too heavy now to carry far. Jody put him down, and he followed Jody into his bedroom. They lay down together. Jody's head was on the fawn's side. Now, he had to have the fawn in his bed. He had a good reason now. Ma couldn't say anything. The danger of bears was a good reason. And there, they fell asleep.

Jody Loses a Friend

*Now he understood. This was death. Death was a silence
and it gave back no answer.*

It was time for Buck to go home. Penny was stronger now and he was able to do a little work.

The earth was hot under the July sun. Jody was hoeing the potatoes, but the fawn wanted to play. He stood in front of Jody and tried to stop him. Jody sent him away. The fawn lay down and watched the boy with his hoe.

The fawn was growing big and was getting into a lot of trouble. One day, he ate all of the cornbread in the kitchen that was ready for supper. At mealtimes, they had to put the fawn in the barn because he tried to take food off their plates.

Ma Baxter wasn't very happy about the fawn, but Jody often said, "Aren't his eyes pretty, Ma?"

"They can see a plate of cornbread real well," she answered.

"Hasn't he got a pretty tail, Ma?"

"They all look the same."

Jody wanted to visit Fodder-wing and ask him for a good name for his fawn. But he still had a lot of hoeing to do.

Penny came out of the house and said, "That's a lot of potatoes, isn't it?"

"Pa, I'll never finish," said Jody.

"You can't walk away from work, son. But, maybe I can help you, if you help me. I'll hoe your potatoes tonight, if you get some water now. I can't carry two big pots of water. My arm isn't strong yet."

Jody dropped the hoe and ran to the house for the water-pots.

Penny called, "Don't try to carry full pots. A **yearling** isn't as strong as a buck."

◆

yearling /'yɪrlɪŋ/ (n) a young animal between the ages of one and two

52

Jody and his fawn reached the Forresters' land and hurried into the open yard. It was quiet.

Jody called, "Fodder-wing! It's Jody!"

A dog cried softly. Buck came to the door. He looked down at Jody. His eyes were open, but he didn't see.

Jody said slowly, "I've come to see Fodder-wing. I've come to show him my fawn."

Buck shook his head, then said, "He's dead."

"What does he mean?" thought Jody. The words went past Jody into the air. He felt a sudden coldness. He didn't understand.

"You've come too late. There was no time to get you . . . or the doctor. He was alive one minute and dead the next minute. It was like a candle going out."

Jody felt cold and weak.

Buck said with difficulty, "You can come in and look at him."

Buck turned to go into the house. He looked over his shoulder and his eyes pulled Jody into the house. The Forrester men sat together like one big rock—heavy and silent. Pa Forrester looked at Jody, then he turned away again. Lem and Mill-wheel looked at him. The others didn't move. Buck held Jody's hand and took him into the large bedroom. He started to speak, but the words didn't come. He stopped and held Jody's shoulder.

"Be strong," he said.

Fodder-wing lay with his eyes closed. He looked small in the center of the large bed. Jody was scared. Ma Forrester sat next to the bed.

She said, "I've lost my boy. My poor little strange-shaped boy." She covered her eyes and cried softly, "Life is hard. Life is so hard."

Jody wanted to run away. Fodder-wing's little face filled him with fear. Buck pulled him to the side of the bed.

"He won't hear, but speak to him," said Buck.

Jody tried, but Fodder-wing's silence was too painful. No words came out of his mouth. But he had to speak, so he tried again. His voice came out.

Now he understood. This was death. Death was a silence and it gave back no answer.

"Fodder-wing will never speak to me again," he thought.

He turned and put his face against Buck's chest. The big arms held him tightly. They stood together for a long time.

Buck said, "It's fearful for you, I know."

Then, they left the room and Jody went outside, to the back of the house. Fodder-wing's pets were there. There were rabbits, squirrels, raccoons, and a little red bird. They didn't have any food or water, so Jody fed them. He played with them for a few minutes. Jody wanted Fodder-wing so much, and it was so painful. He looked for his fawn. When he found him, he felt some small amount of happiness.

Jody stayed because the Forresters wanted him there. The men came out of the house and fed their animals and did their work.

"I can help you, Buck," Jody said.

"There are plenty of us to do the work. You can sit with Ma like Fodder-wing always did. Keep her fire going."

Ma Forrester was standing by the fire. Her eyes were red.

Jody said, "I've come to help."

Jody felt uncomfortable, but he couldn't leave. Ma Forrester made some dinner, but there wasn't much.

The men came in and sat down at the table. Ma Forrester put meat on the plates and sat down. Then she began to cry again.

"I put down a plate for him, the same as always."

Buck said, "Jody'll eat it, Ma . . . and maybe he'll grow up as big as me."

The men ate for a few minutes, then pushed away their plates.

Ma Forrester said to Jody, "You didn't eat your potatoes or drink your milk."

"That's for my fawn. I always give him some of my dinner."

She said, "You poor little thing." She began to cry again. "My boy loved animals. He talked and talked about your fawn. He wanted to see it."

Jody said with difficulty, "I came here to show Fodder-wing my fawn. I wanted Fodder-wing to give him a good name."

"He . . . he named it," said Ma Forrester. "I remember Fodder-wing saying, 'A fawn carries its tail up like a **flag**. Jody can name him Flag.'"

Jody repeated, "Flag."

Jody's heart was full of happiness and great sadness—both at the same time.

---

flag /flæg/ (n) a piece of cloth with different colors on it; every country has a *flag*

CHAPTER 11

Trouble at Baxter's Island

Penny saw Slewfoot's tracks and he was very angry. "I'll get that bear. This time, it's me or him."

In early fall, the corn and potato plants were destroyed by heavy rains. Many animals were killed, too.

Penny had to work hard to save the rest of the corn and potatoes. Jody worked many hours to help him. So, when Flag knocked over a pile of potatoes, he was in big trouble. He stepped on them and bit into them. Ma Baxter was very angry when she discovered the mess. When Jody saw his father's face, he started to cry.

He said, "He didn't know he was being bad, Pa."

"I know that," said Penny, "but the result is the same. We won't have enough to eat."

"I won't eat any potatoes," said Jody.

"That's not what we want. But you have to watch Flag so he doesn't get into trouble."

That wasn't easy to do.

◆

There were problems with Lem Forrester again, too. Lem wanted to fight all the time, and he attacked Penny one day.

"Penny lied," he told his brothers. It was about a buck that Lem wanted. "Penny killed it and tried to keep it for himself. He told me not to kill it. Then, he got it."

The brothers believed Lem and they didn't want to see Penny again.

Ma Baxter said, "I'm happy that they don't want to talk to us now."

Penny answered, "Don't forget how Buck helped us."

"I haven't forgotten. But Lem is like a rattlesnake. He'll attack you because he's heard something move in the trees."

But one day in December, Buck visited the Baxters. The Forresters were having a lot of trouble from old Slewfoot. He was going to their place and killing their calves. Penny was grateful for the information and thanked Buck.

"You're not angry about that deer, I hope," said Penny.

"Don't worry about it. What's one deer?" said Buck.

Buck left, and Penny felt unhappy. He wanted to be friendly with his only neighbors.

In December, there wasn't a lot of work. Jody spent many hours with Flag. The fawn was growing fast. Almost every day, Jody took his gun and went to the woods with Flag.

Soon it was the week before Christmas. The Baxters were very happy because Trixie's calf was born. Now, they didn't have to spend Christmas at home—they could go to Volusia for the Christmas party. Trixie's milk was for the new calf, so Penny didn't have to think about his cow.

Four days before Christmas, Buck visited the Baxters again. Old Slewfoot was still killing their animals. Penny thanked Buck for telling him. That night, Penny prepared to catch the thief.

But the next morning, when Penny went to the barn, the calf wasn't there. Penny saw Slewfoot's tracks and he was very angry.

"I'll get that bear. This time, it's me or him."

Ma Baxter hurriedly put cornbread and potatoes into a bag while Penny and Jody got their guns. Penny took the dogs and Jody took Flag. A mile to the west, they found the dead calf.

They followed Slewfoot's tracks, walking very quickly. They stopped for only a few minutes to eat their food and to rest. In the afternoon, Jody was very tired and the dogs were, too. Only Flag played and ran happily.

Jody asked Penny, "Aren't you tired, Pa?"

"I don't get tired when I'm so mad," said Penny.

At dark, they returned to Baxter's Island. But the next morning, they got up very early.

Penny said to Jody, "You can come with me, but this is not going to be fun. It's cold and it'll be really difficult. I'm not coming home until I get that bear. Do you want to go or not?"

"Yes," Jody answered.

Ma Baxter looked at the new dress that she had for the Christmas party.

"Ezra, tomorrow is the day before Christmas," she told her husband.

"Maybe I'll be here and maybe I won't. You can take the horse and go to Volusia tomorrow. Maybe I'll see you there. That's the best that I can do."

6.1 Were you right?

Look back at your answers to Activity 5.4. Then complete the sentences.

Jody takes his fawn to the Forresters' house to show him to
¹.. . But when he gets there, Buck gives him the sad
news that ².. is ³.. . At the
side of his friend's body, Jody finally understands ⁴.. .
He sits with ⁵.. and eats with the family. He learns
that Fodder-wing named Jody's fawn ⁶.. .

6.2 What more did you learn?

1 Match the animals with the food that they steal or destroy.

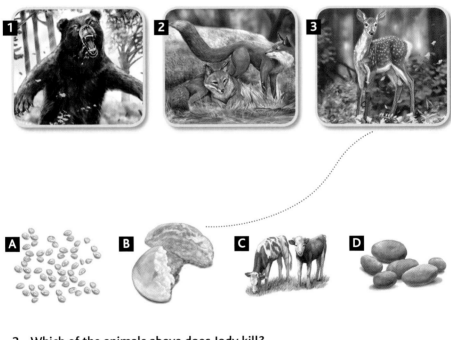

2 Which of the animals above does Jody kill?

....

3 Have the problems between the Baxters and the Forresters finished?

....

6.3 Language in use

Look at the sentences in the box. Then complete the sentences below.

> The corn and potato plants **were destroyed** by heavy rains. Many animals **were killed**, too.

1 The corn .... _was planted_ .... (plant) by Buck, but then it ....
   .... (steal) by foxes.

2 The foxes .... (shoot) by Jody.

3 The fawn .... (keep) in the barn at night.

4 Flag .... (give) his name by Fodder-wing.

5 The Baxters .... (tell) about the disappearance of
   the Forresters' calves.

6 Trixie's calf .... (find) a mile from the Baxters'
   house.

6.4 What happens next?

What do you think? What happens at the end of the story? Complete the sentences with these names.

| Jody | Flag | Penny | Lem | Grandma Hutto | Oliver |

1 .... _Penny_ .... kills Slewfoot.

2 .... helps to carry the dead bear back to Baxter's Island.

3 .... is married to Twink Weatherby.

4 .... 's house is burned down.

5 .... destroys half of Penny's tobacco plants.

6 .... kills Flag.

CHAPTER 12

Christmas Surprises

*Slewfoot was standing there and ready to fight. The dogs
jumped and bit the great bear. It fought angrily.*

Penny was silent because he was so full of hate. Jody followed him as Julia followed the tracks. It was a long day, without success. That night, they slept in a little house in the woods. It belonged to Nellie Ginright—an old friend of Penny's. The next morning, Nellie made breakfast for Penny and Jody. She was a woman like Grandma Hutto, and Jody liked her. She and Penny laughed and talked. Jody was happy to see his father smile again. After breakfast, she gave them some food, and they left.

It was the day before Christmas and Jody wanted to go to the party in Volusia, but he couldn't ask Penny. It was more important to kill Slewfoot. They followed the bear's tracks all morning. At noon, Julia started barking in her special way. Slewfoot was standing there and ready to fight. The dogs jumped and bit the great bear. It fought angrily. Penny shot at it. Old Slewfoot fell to the ground.

Jody felt weak as he and Penny walked toward the dead bear.

"I am surprised," said Penny. Then, he shouted happily and laughed. Jody and Penny danced around Slewfoot, and sang.

Penny took out his knife to clean the bear. Jody helped. Then, they tried to pull the heavy body, but it was impossible.

"We won't get to the river before spring!" laughed Penny.

"What'll we do?" asked Jody.

"We'll have to walk to Fort Gates and ask someone to help us."

They started walking. Penny told Jody a funny story about his Uncle Miles. They were laughing when suddenly they heard horses. The riders were the Forresters. They were laughing loudly and passing a bottle around.

"Penny Baxter, what are you doing here?"

"I've been hunting. Jody and I came out to get old Slewfoot."

"Do you hear that, boys?"

"And we got him. He's dead."

The Forresters couldn't hide their surprise.

"Jody and I are going to Fort Gates to get help. We can't carry that bear—only the two of us."

Lem asked, "What'll you give us if we carry him out?"

"Half of the meat. I was planning to give you half because Slewfoot killed so many of your animals. I'm grateful to Buck for telling me."

Buck sat up straight and said, "You and me are friends, Penny Baxter. Get up here behind me and show me the way. When we finish, we'll go to Volusia for the Christmas party."

Penny got on Buck's horse and Jody got on Mill-wheel's. Penny didn't like the idea of the Forresters at the party. But there was nothing that he could do.

The bear weighed about four hundred pounds, so they cut it into four pieces. Buck didn't want to cut it up, because he wanted everybody to see its great size. But Penny didn't agree. After much discussion, Buck listened to Penny.

They arrived at Baxter's Island after dark. Ma wasn't there and the house was dark. Jody called for Flag, but Flag didn't come. Jody was afraid. He called again. This time, Flag came running. Jody wanted to take him to Volusia, but he couldn't. So, he put him in the barn and gave him some food.

The Forresters went to Volusia with Penny and Jody. Buck took the bear skin. He put it on before he walked into the party at the church. Some women screamed when they saw him.

"Take it off, Buck—or someone will shoot you," Penny said.

Most of the men and boys stood around Penny and listened to the story about the hunt. Ory greeted him, then went and got a plate of food for her husband. The men were excited and asked a lot of questions.

There were great piles of food, and the church looked very pretty. Grandma Hutto gave Jody a lot of different cakes.

Ma Baxter said, "If you eat all of those cakes, you won't eat any meat or bread."

"I don't want any," said Jody happily.

Grandma Hutto said, "Don't worry, Ory. He can eat cornbread for the rest of the year."

Jody looked at his mother. She looked pretty in her new dress and she was proud of her husband. "It's a great thing to be Penny Baxter's family," he thought.

The Forrester men stood together near the church door. One brave woman took some food to them. The other women didn't want to go near them. They were drinking with some of the men, and their voices were louder than the rest of the party. Then, the music started and some of the men asked women to dance. Buck, Mill-wheel, and Gabby were dancing with three young girls. Lem watched.

Grandma Hutto sat down and said, "I didn't know they were coming—those black-beards!"

"Of course, *I* didn't know," said Ma Baxter angrily.

It was the first time that the two women agreed.

The church door opened and a stranger walked in. Lem Forrester spoke to him. Then, Lem said something to his brothers. A minute later, the Forresters went out together.

CHAPTER 13

A Mother's Love

As they were near Grandma Hutto's house, they saw a great fire. Grandma Hutto's house was burning.

The stranger was given some food. He was stopping in Volusia on his way up the river.

"Some other passengers got off here," he said. "Maybe you know them—Mr. Oliver Hutto and a young lady."

Grandma Hutto stood up.

"Oliver Hutto? Are you sure of that name?"

"Yes. His home is here—he told me. It's over in that direction," the stranger said, pointing toward Grandma Hutto's.

Penny hurried toward Grandma Hutto and said, "The Forresters have probably gone to your house. Do you want to come with me?"

Jody and Ma Baxter followed Penny and Grandma Hutto. As they were near Grandma Hutto's house, they saw a great fire. Grandma Hutto's house was burning.

Grandma called, "Oliver! Oliver!"

She ran toward the house. Penny pulled her back and said, "Do you want to die?"

"Oliver's there! Oliver! Oliver!"

Penny could see the tracks in the sand. There was no question. The tracks belonged to the Forresters' horses. Penny told Jody to get on Caesar and go to Boyles' store. Maybe Mr. Boyles knew where Oliver was. Maybe he saw him and Twink when they got off the boat.

Jody was afraid. His hands were like wood, but he got on the horse and rode away. A man and woman were walking down the road toward the river. He heard the man laugh.

He shouted, "Oliver!" and jumped down.

"Hi, Jody!" said Oliver.

"Oliver, Grandma's house is burning down! The Forresters did it!"

Grandma Hutto's face changed to great happiness when she saw her son.

"Which way did those Forresters go?" asked Oliver.

Grandma stood up straight and said, "Why do you want the Forresters?"

"They did it—Jody said." Oliver answered angrily.

"Jody, you silly boy. I left a candle burning by an open window. That's what did it. Jody, do you want another fight here?"

Jody was surprised. His mother's mouth was wide open.

Penny looked at Grandma Hutto. Then, he said, "Yes, son, you know that the Forresters are miles away."

Oliver said, "I'm glad. I don't want to kill Forresters tonight." He looked at Twink and at the others and said, "Meet my wife."

Grandma Hutto was surprised, but she walked to the girl and kissed her. Oliver took Twink's hand and they walked around the burning house.

Grandma looked at the Baxters and said, "I don't want Forresters' blood and my son's body lying on the ground—not for a house."

Penny held her in his arms. Oliver and Twink returned.

"We'll build another house for you, Ma. Don't worry," said Oliver.

"I don't want it. I'm too old. I want to live in Boston."

Jody looked at his father. Penny looked tired and sad.

"I want to go in the morning," Grandma Hutto continued.

Oliver said, "My boat always leaves from Boston, Ma. I'll see you more often!"

CHAPTER 14

Gone For Ever

"He's not the baby that you brought home," said Penny.
"He's a yearling now."

Life was very quiet in January. Grandma Hutto, Oliver, and Twink were gone. The Forresters stayed away. Then, in February, Penny was sick, so Jody had to do a lot of the work. When he finished, he played with Flag. Flag was almost a yearling, and a lot of yearlings were shot for food. Jody knew this.

"Pa, do you think that Flag is a yearling now?"

"I think that he'll be a yearling in about a month."

"How will he be different?" Jody asked.

"He'll stay in the woods more and grow a lot bigger."

But Flag began to be in serious trouble. He was too big to be in the house. Ma Baxter was often very angry with him. But the worst thing happened when he destroyed half of Penny's tobacco plants.

"He was jumping and playing," Penny said. "He didn't do it to be bad. But now I haven't got enough tobacco to sell to Mr. Boyles. You have to build a fence, Jody. I'll give you some wood."

Jody felt worse because Penny was so kind.

Jody worked very hard to build the fence. "Now Flag can't destroy any more of Pa's tobacco plants," Jody hoped.

◆

It was March and time to plant the corn. Jody and Penny worked all day. As they finished, Flag came running toward them. He ran around them, then stopped to eat.

"Look at his long neck, Pa," said Jody.

Penny watched Flag. Jody saw something in his father's face, something strange. He didn't know what his father was thinking.

"Pa?" Jody said.

"He's not the baby that you brought home," said Penny. "He's a yearling now."

Penny's words didn't give Jody much happiness.

A few weeks later, Penny asked Jody to look at the corn. "See if it's coming up yet," said Penny.

Jody looked, but he couldn't see any corn. He walked closer. Flag's tracks were in the ground and the corn was gone. Jody went back to the house with slow, heavy feet and sat down.

"Son, how's the corn?"

Jody could hear his own heart. "Something ate it," he answered.

Penny was silent. At last, he spoke. "Couldn't you see what ate it?"

Jody looked at his father. His eyes were asking Penny to say nothing more.

"I'll ask your Ma to look. She can tell."

"Don't send Ma!" shouted Jody.

"She'll know."

"Don't send her!"

"Flag did it, didn't he?"

"Yes, sir."

Penny felt very sorry for his son. "I'm sorry, boy. Go out and play. Tell your Ma to come here."

"Don't tell her, Pa. Please don't tell her."

"She has to know, Jody. Now, go outside. I'll do the best that I can for you."

Jody walked slowly into the kitchen. "Pa wants you, Ma."

◆

Penny decided to give Flag one more try, and Ory had to agree. They told Jody to build another fence—a very high fence. Jody loved Flag and he wanted to keep him, but Flag had to stay out of the corn and tobacco. So, Jody got up very early every morning to work on the fence. After a few days, he had dark circles under his eyes. Penny wanted to help his son, but he had too much other work. On the sixth day, Ma Baxter went out and helped Jody. Jody was surprised, but grateful. That night, Jody discovered the new corn plants breaking through the ground.

The next day, Jody finished the south and east ends and was starting on the north. Ma was still helping. The fence was eight feet high. Suddenly, Jody noticed Flag's tracks. His heart stopped. The new corn was gone again!

Ma was angrier than before. She hurried into the house. Jody followed and went to his bed. He lay down, prepared for trouble. But he wasn't prepared for the impossible, or for his father's words.

Penny said, "Jody, we have done everything that was possible. I'm sorry. Flag cannot destroy our year's plants. We have to eat. Take the yearling out in the woods and tie him and shoot him."

Suddenly, they heard a shot. Jody ran and opened the kitchen door. His mother was holding the gun in her arms. Flag was lying on the ground, but still moving, by the fence. Jody ran to Flag. The yearling got up on his three good legs and tried to run.

"Go, finish him, Jody. He's in pain," shouted Penny.

Jody took the gun from his mother. He screamed, "You always hated him."

Flag ran and fell. Jody cried, "It's me! It's me! Flag!"

He stood above the dying animal and put the gun to its neck and shot Flag. He threw the gun down and fell flat to the ground. He was sick. He kicked and screamed.

Jody stayed away for three days. He was hungry, tired, and alone. But he needed to think. Then, he decided he had to go home. He wanted to see his father and talk to him. He needed him.

When Jody walked into the house, Penny took his hand. He held it between his own two hands.

Penny said, "You've learned a lesson. You aren't a yearling now. Life isn't easy, Jody. I wanted life to be easy for you. I wanted you to have fun with your yearling. But, in the end, every man is alone. When he's knocked down, he has to get up."

"I know that now, Pa," said Jody.

Penny gave his son some food and they talked. Then Penny went to bed and Jody went to his room and closed the door.

"Flag won't be there in the morning when I go out for milk," Jody thought. He lay in his bed, listening. He was listening for the sound of the yearling and thought, "I'll never hear him again. I'll never love anything as much as I loved him. I'll be lonely all of my life. But that's how it is for a man."

In the beginning of his sleep, he cried out, "Flag!"

It wasn't his own voice that called. It was a boy's voice. Somewhere in the woods, a boy and a yearling ran side by side, and were gone for ever.

Talk about it

1 Work in pairs. It is the day after the Christmas party in Volusia. Have this
conversation.

| Student A: | You are Lem Forrester. You are angry with the Baxters. Tell your brother why. |

| Student B: | You are Buck Forrester. You don't want trouble between your family and the Baxters. You think the Baxters are good people. Tell your brother why. |

2 Work in pairs. It is twenty years after the end of the story. Have this
conversation.

| Student A: | You are Jody's son. You want a pet. Ask for one, and ask questions about your father's pet fawn. |

| Student B: | You are Jody. Tell your son about your pet fawn. Then decide: can your son have a pet or not? Explain your reasons. |

3 Think about yourself, your family, and your friends. Has anyone had similar
problems to Jody's? Think about trouble with neighbors, fights over
girlfriends/boyfriends, and problems with pets. Make notes below, and then
discuss what happened.

Notes

You are Jody. Complete this letter to Grandma Hutto, a year after the start of the story. Put in:

- questions about her new life in Boston, and about Oliver and Twink
- what happened to Flag
- memories of the other bad things that happened last year
- news of your parents, the Forresters, and the animals and plants on the farm.

Baxter's Island

Florida

April 24th

Dear Grandma Hutto,

Project *Staying Alive*

WORK WITH TWO OR THREE OTHER STUDENTS.

1. **In the story, Penny almost dies from a rattlesnake bite. The natural world is a dangerous place. Write a list of other ways in which the natural world can kill you.**

> You are caught in an electric storm
> A bear attacks you in the woods

2. **Read Kath Levin's story and then have the conversation below.**

I was walking in the mountains with some friends. Suddenly snow started to fall down the mountainside. It was very frightening. We held onto a tree, but the snow carried me down the hill. I pulled the neck of my T-shirt up over my face and kept my mouth closed. I fell for a long time and the snow covered me. I made an air space around my mouth. Then I kicked hard, and got near the top of the snow. I pushed my hand up until the tops of my fingers were above the snow. But then I couldn't move. I waited and waited. It was so cold! After half an hour, I heard my friends shouting. I shouted back, and soon they found me.

| **Students A–C:** | You are Kath's friends. You have just saved her. Ask her how she is. Find out how she stayed alive. |
| **Student D:** | You are Kath. Answer your friends' questions. |

3 Talk about the dangers of the natural world in movies, books, or TV shows. What happens to the people in stories like these? Do they die? If not, what do they do to stay alive?

4 Read the sentences below. Which information sheet do you think they are from? Write A or B.

A # BIG CATS
How to stay alive!

B ## A WALKER'S GUIDE
How to stay alive in an electric storm!

1 ☐B Keep away from open fields. You don't want to be the tallest thing in the area.

2 ☐ Never go near babies. Mothers often attack to protect their children.

3 ☐ Don't make fast or sudden movements. Always move slowly.

4 ☐ If a big cat bites you, pull hard on its biggest lower teeth.

5 ☐ If you are carrying metal things, put them at least six meters away from you.

6 ☐ Don't wait under a single tree. You'll be safer in a space between a group of trees.

7 ☐ If you are losing a lot of blood from a bite, burn your skin with red-hot metal.

8 ☐ Make your body into a ball. Keep your feet together, with only your toes touching the ground. Close your eyes. Put your hands over your ears to protect them from the noise.

5 Your group is going to make an information sheet about staying alive. Choose a danger of the natural world. Find information on the Internet. Plan and write something that you can put on the wall.